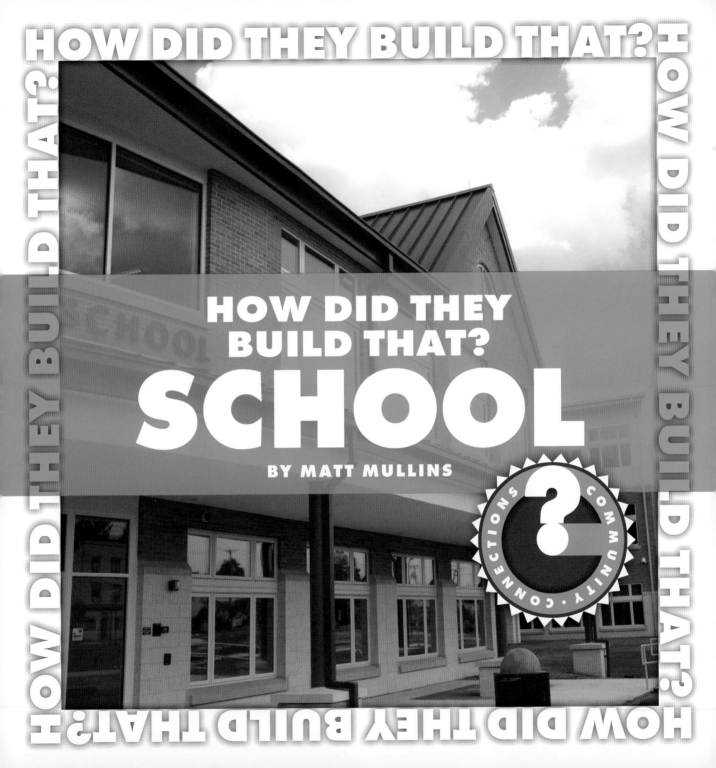

HOW DID THEY BUILD THAT?
SCHOOL

BY MATT MULLINS

Published in the United States of America by Cherry Lake Publishing
Ann Arbor, Michigan
www.cherrylakepublishing.com

Content Adviser: Nancy Kristof
Reading Adviser: Cecilia Minden-Cupp, PhD, Literacy Consultant

Photo Credits: Cover and page 1, ©iStockphoto.com/deystudio; page 5, ©iStockphoto.com/RapidEye; page 7, ©Ca2hill/Dreamstime.com; page 9, ©iStockphoto.com/MICHELANGELOBOY; page 11, ©Christina Richards, used under license from Shutterstock, Inc.; page 13, ©iStockphoto.com/millraw; page 15, ©Brad Sauter, used under license from Shutterstock, Inc.; page 17, ©Rob Byron, used under license from Shutterstock, Inc.; page 19, ©Monkeybusinessimages/Dreamstime.com; page 21, ©Orhancam/Dreamstime.com

LIBRARY OF CONGRESS CATALOGING-IN-PUBLICATION DATA
Mullins, Matt.
  How did they build that? School / by Matt Mullins.
     p. cm.—(Community connections)
  Includes index.
  ISBN-13: 978-1-60279-487-0
  ISBN-10: 1-60279-487-1
  1. Schools—Design and construction—Juvenile literature.
  2. School buildings—Design and construction—Juvenile literature.
  I. Title II. Series.
  LB3205.M85 2010
  711'.57—dc22   2008047975

Cherry Lake Publishing would like to acknowledge the work of The Partnership for 21st Century Skills. Please visit *www.21stcenturyskills.org* for more information.

CONTENTS

WHAT'S IN A SCHOOL?

Building a school is like building a big house. Except this building has a **cafeteria** and a library. Don't forget the gym and playground!

Building a school is a big job. It is just like other big building projects. Construction work starts with the land.

Some people plan what a new school building will look like.

5

PREPARING THE LAND

First, you have to find a good space to build the school. The space must be big enough to fit all the rooms. Trees may need to be cut down. Dirt will be scraped flat.

Special machines make it possible to move big piles of dirt.

It costs a lot of money to build a school. What parts of the school do you think cost the most to build? Ask your principal or your teacher what they think.

7

Bulldozers clear the land. These giant tractors have a big blade in front that looks like a wall. The blade shoves away objects and bumps in the land. Special machines dig **trenches** for water and sewer pipes. Now building can begin!

Machines dig trenches to make space for pipes and cables in the ground.

LOOK!

Look around outside your school. What plants do you see? Can you tell which plants were there before the school was built? Can you tell which ones were planted after the school was built? How can you tell the difference?

FOUNDATIONS AND FRAMES

A big building needs a place to sit. This seat has to be strong and hard. It must hold the building steady. This hard seat is called the **foundation**.

Foundations are made from **concrete**. Concrete is a gray mixture of sand, gravel, water, and **cement**.

It takes a lot of concrete to make a strong foundation.

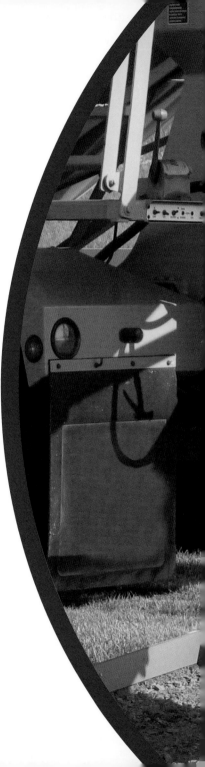

Workers pour concrete while it's wet. It is poured into the exact place that they want the foundation. Concrete becomes hard and strong when it dries.

Workers build the school's **frame** after the concrete dries. Then the frame is covered with walls, floors, and ceilings.

12

Builders work as a team to make the frame of a building.

Mix dirt with some water to make a thick mud. Use the mud as "concrete" to build a small wall. You need to use just enough water to turn the mud into clay. The wall should get hard when the mud dries.

13

SPECIAL ROOMS

Schools have many classrooms. They also have other rooms. One room is the gym. It is for games and sports. Many gyms have wood floors. Others have floors made of plastic or tile. Sometimes workers put rubber or foam under the floor. This makes it safer. It also makes it better for running and jumping.

Many school gyms are big, open spaces with high ceilings.

The school cafeteria is another room found in many schools. Kids eat lunch there. It needs to be big enough to hold many big tables. Some cafeterias have large kitchens. Workers put in big ovens for baking. They put in big refrigerators, too. Some cafeteria kitchens have big dishwashers.

Does your school cafeteria look like this?

A school building also has a library. Workers build many shelves for books.

Other workers put in electric and phone wires. The wires are needed to run the lights and computers. Schools have lights in every room. Some school libraries have many computers.

Some libraries have rooms where students can study in groups.

Guess how many books are in your school library. Guess how many different magazines the library has. Write down your guesses. Now ask your librarian for the answers. Were your guesses close to the actual number?

19

BRING IN THE STUDENTS!

When the school buildings are completed, workers finish the school grounds. Playgrounds are a favorite part of the school grounds. Some schools also have beautiful **landscaping**.

Now the new school is ready. Bring in the students!

The best playgrounds are both fun and safe to use.

THINK!

The most important part of the playground is the ground cover. Some play areas are covered with sand. Some are covered with tiny round rocks called pea gravel. Why do you think playgrounds have these kinds of ground cover?

21

GLOSSARY

bulldozers (BUHL-doh-zuhrz) heavy machines with a blade in front for moving land

cafeteria (kaf-uh-TIHR-ee-uh) an area for eating

cement (suh-MENT) a gray powder made from crushed limestone that is mixed with water and left to dry until it hardens; one of the ingredients needed to make concrete

concrete (KON-kreet) strong building material made from cement, sand, gravel, and water

foundation (foun-DAY-shuhn) a base on which something stands or is built

frame (FRAYM) the parts of a building or structure that give it shape

landscaping (LAND-skape-ing) decorating or improving an area of land with plants, flowers, trees, and soil

trenches (TREHNCH-ez) long, narrow ditches

FIND OUT MORE

BOOKS

C Is for Construction: Big Trucks and Diggers from A to Z. San Francisco: Chronicle Books, 2003.

Nevius, Carol. *Building with Dad.* Tarrytown, NY: Marshall Cavendish, 2006.

WEB SITES

Kids-n-Fun.com—Coloring Pages: Machines
www.kids-n-fun.com/coloringpages/kleurplaat_Machines_136.aspx
Pictures of bulldozers and other big construction machines to download and color

Playground Safety for Kids!
www.kidchecker.org/main.htm
Learn more about what makes playgrounds safe for kids and how to stay safe on the playground

23

INDEX

ABOUT THE AUTHOR

Matt Mullins lives with his wife and son in Madison, Wisconsin. Formerly a journalist, Matt writes about science and engineering, current affairs, food and wine, and anything else that draws his interest.